MUSHROOMS

MUSHROOMS

by Sylvia A. Johnson

Photographs by Masana Izawa

A Lerner Natural Science Book

Lerner Publications Company ▪ Minneapolis

Sylvia A. Johnson, Series Editor

Translation of original text by Chaim Uri

The publisher wishes to thank Robert Blanchette,
Assistant Professor, Department of Plant Pathology, University of Minnesota,
and Eddie P. Hill, Professor of Biology, Macalester College,
for their assistance in the preparation of this book.

Drawings on pages 9, 17, 22, and 37 by Yoshikazu Natsume
Photograph on page 20 from Carolina Biological Supply Company

An explanation of the scientific names used in this book appears on page 44. The glossary on page 46 gives definitions and pronunciations of words shown in **bold type** in the text.

LIBRARY OF CONGRESS CATALOGING IN PUBLICATION DATA

Johnson, Sylvia A.
  Mushrooms.

    (A Lerner natural science book)
    Adaptation of: Kinoko no sekai/Masana Izawa.
    Includes index.
    Summary: Discusses how mushrooms and other fungi get their food, grow, and produce more of their own kind.
      1. Mushrooms—Juvenile literature. [1. Mushrooms. 2. Fungi] I. Izawa, Masana, ill. II. Izawa, Masana. Kinoko no sekai. III. Title. IV. Series.

  QK617.J64   589.2   82-212
  ISBN 0-8225-1473-7 (lib. bdg.)   AACR2

International Standard Book Number: 0-8225-1473-7
Library of Congress Catalog Card Number: 82-212

   2   3   4   5   6   7   8   9   10   91   90   89   88   87   86   85   84   83

What do you think the object in this photograph is? It looks like a tiny umbrella with a delicate silk shade, but it is actually a mushroom, shown enlarged to about six times its real size. This beautiful little plant is one of the many kinds of mushrooms that grow in fields and forests throughout the world.

Mushrooms are part of a larger group of plants known as **fungi,** a group that also includes molds and mildews. A fungus is different from an ordinary green plant because it cannot make its own food. In this book, you will find out how mushrooms and other fungi get their food, grow, and produce more of their own kind.

The scaly cluster fungus (*Pholiota adiposa*) has rough scales on its cap and stalk. (Shown about one-half actual size.)

Mushrooms come in many different shapes, sizes, and colors, and they grow in many different places. The pictures on these two pages show a few of the more than 38,000 kinds of mushrooms. (The names used to describe the mushrooms are explained on page 44.)

Left: Coral mushrooms like *Ramaria Botrytis* have many branches and stalks that resemble the coral found in tropical oceans. Right: This species (*Lactarius volemus*) belongs to a group known as milk mushrooms because they produce a milky liquid when cut or broken. (Both shown actual size.)

Above: The brick cap mushroom *(Nae-matoloma sublateritium)* gets its common name from the brick-red color on the center of its cap. (One-half actual size) Right: This delicate green mushroom is a member of the large group known as earth tongues. (Actual size)

Left: The bird's nest mushroom *(Cyathus striatus)* looks just like its common name. This little mushroom is no bigger than a pea. Right: The large beefsteak fungus *(Fistulina hepatica)* belongs to a group known as shelf fungi, usually found growing on trees.

Left: These mushroom fruiting bodies are growing among dead leaves on the forest floor. Right: Hidden under the leaves is the mushroom mycelium, the mass of thread-like structures that produced the fruiting bodies.

The colorful umbrellas, branches, shelves, and cups that we call mushrooms are actually only one small part of a mushroom plant. The rest of the plant is hidden beneath the surface on which the mushroom grows. The hidden part of a mushroom is called the **mycelium;** it is made up of a mass of thread-like structures known as **hyphae.** The mycelium of a mushroom is the part of the plant that takes in nourishment and grows larger. It can be compared to the roots, stems, and leaves of green plants.

When the mycelium has grown to a certain point, it produces the part of the mushroom that can be seen above the surface. This part is known as the **fruiting body** because it plays the same role as the fruit does in the growth of a green plant. It contains the material that will eventually produce new mushroom plants.

8

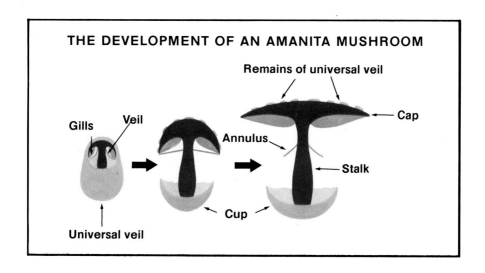

THE DEVELOPMENT OF AN AMANITA MUSHROOM

Remains of universal veil

Gills Veil Cap Annulus Stalk Cup Universal veil

When the fruiting body of a mushroom first appears, it looks like a tiny button pushing its way above the surface. The developing mushroom is well protected as it grows into its adult form. In most of the familiar umbrella-shaped mushrooms, the young fruiting body has a thin skin called a **veil** that protects the underside of the umbrella, or **cap.** As the fruiting body grows larger, this veil splits. The remains of the veil often form a ring or **annulus** on the stalk of the mushroom, below the cap.

Mushrooms that belong to the genus *Amanita* have a special kind of covering in the button stage. In addition to the veil on the underside of the cap, there is a larger **universal veil** that encloses the whole fruiting body. This veil also splits as the mushroom grows, leaving behind a kind of cup at the base of the stalk. Parts of the veil also remain on the top of the cap, where they appear as little scales or warts.

The mushrooms shown on these two pages are members of the genus *Amanita.* You can see the cups at the bottom of the stalks and the warts on the caps that are typical of mushrooms in this group. Such characteristics make the Amanitas fairly easy to recognize, which is fortunate since many of these mushrooms contain a deadly poison. (All of the Amanitas shown on this page are extremely poisonous if eaten.)

Destroying angel *(Amanita virosa)*

Right: Fly Amanita *(Amanita muscaria)* Below: Panther Amanita *(Amanita pantherina)*

This beautiful mushroom is known as Caesar's Amanita (*Amanita caesarea*). Unlike many of its relatives, it is not poisonous.

Amanita mushrooms are part of a large group known as gilled mushrooms. Members of this group, which includes many of the familiar umbrella-type mushrooms, have tiny, deep ridges called **gills** on the undersides of their caps. These gills play an important part in the production of new mushroom plants.

New mushrooms grow from **spores,** tiny cells that are produced by the fruiting bodies of mature mushroom plants. The fruiting body of a mushroom can produce millions of spores at one time. A single spore is so small that it cannot be seen without a microscope. Many spores together look like fine powder or dust.

A gilled mushroom manufactures spores within tiny club-shaped bodies that cover the surface of the gills. Each little club produces four spores. When the spores are ripe, they are shot out of the clubs, away from the surface of the gills. Once they are free from the gills, the spores drift away on the wind.

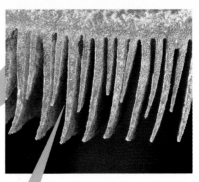

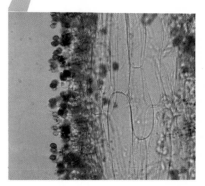

The mushroom's gills magnified 5 times

This microscopic view of the surface of a gill shows the tiny black spores magnified 200 times.

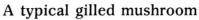

A typical gilled mushroom

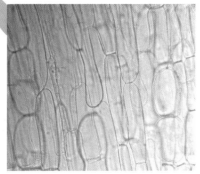

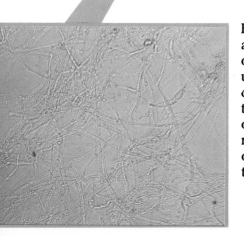

Both the mycelium (left) and the fruiting body (right) of the mushroom are made up of thread-like rows of cells called hyphae. In these pictures, the hyphae of the mycelium are magnified 100 times and those of the fruiting body, 200 times.

13

The sulfur tuft *(Naematoloma fasciculare)* is a gilled mushroom that often grows in large clusters on tree stumps or logs.

One of the most familiar gilled mushrooms is the common table mushroom *(Agaricus bisporus).* Millions of these mushrooms are grown on mushroom farms and sold as food. If you take a close look at a table mushroom, you can see the annulus on the stalk and the tiny, delicate gills on the underside of the white cap.

Among the more exotic gilled mushrooms are the inky caps (opposite). Many of the mushrooms in this group have very unusual habits of growth. Spores develop on the surface of the gills, as they do in other gilled mushrooms.

This species of inky cap
—*Coprinus comatus*—is
sometimes called shaggy
mane because of the
rough scales on its tall,
narrow cap. As the mush-
room matures, its gills
and most of its cap dis-
solve into a black fluid
that looks like ink.

As the inky cap's spores
are released, however, the
mushroom produces a sub-
stance that begins to dissolve
the gills. The gills melt away
in an inky black fluid that
gives this mushroom its common name.

There are many kinds of mushrooms that do not have gills on their fruiting bodies. One group has little holes called **pores** on the areas where spores are produced. In this group are mushrooms in the genus *Boletus.* Boletus mushrooms have caps and stalks like the gilled mushrooms, but the undersides of the caps are covered with thousands of tiny pores rather than gills. The openings lead to little tubes lined with material containing spore-producing bodies. When the spores are ripe, they are shot out of the pores and are carried away on the wind.

Another group of mushrooms with pores are the shelf or bracket mushrooms. These strange-looking plants have no stalks or caps. As their name suggests, they resemble shelves sticking out from the trees on which they grow. The undersides of the shelves are covered with pores.

The spore-producing area of another kind of mushroom is covered with tiny, pointed teeth. Mushrooms in the genus *Hydnum* have short, fine teeth on the undersides of their caps. Other teethed mushrooms grow on trees like the shelf mushrooms and have long teeth hanging down from their lower surfaces.

Mushrooms with teeth, pores, or gills have one major feature in common: they produce spores on the surface of their fruiting bodies. Because of this characteristic, these mushrooms can be studied by means of **spore prints.**

Below: The gills of this unusual mushroom *(Schizophyllum commune)* are split in two. In dry weather, the two sides of the gills curl up to protect the spore-producing surface.

Shelf mushrooms (top) and mushrooms in the genus *Boletus* (center) have little holes on the surfaces where spores are produced. Mushrooms in the genus *Hydnum* (bottom) have fine teeth on their spore-producing surfaces.

17

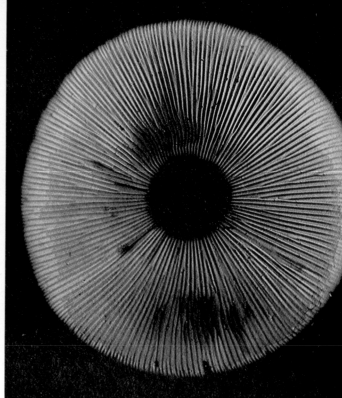

A spore print of an Amanita mushroom

A spore print is made by placing the spore-producing surface of a mature mushroom on a piece of paper. The spores will come off on the paper, revealing a distinctive pattern and color. Scientists can identify many kinds of mushrooms by looking at the prints they make.

The pictures on this page show a gilled mushroom being prepared for a print. First, a damp piece of cotton is placed on the mushroom cap to keep it from drying out (1). Then a glass cover is put over the cap to protect it from drafts of air (2). Three or four hours later, the cap is lifted to reveal the spore print (3).

Spore prints of a Boletus (above) and a coral mushroom (below)

A puffball mushroom releases its spores through the hole at the top of its round fruiting body.

There are large numbers of mushrooms that cannot be used to make spore prints because their spore-producing parts are hidden inside their fruiting bodies. Mushrooms in this group, which includes puffballs, earthstars, and stink-horns, have many fascinating ways of releasing their spores.

The mushroom called the puffball has a ball-shaped fruiting body. Its spores are produced inside the ball, in a structure called a **spore mass**. When the spores are ripe, an opening develops at the top of the ball. If the puffball is touched, even by a drop of rain, its walls squeeze together and the ripe spores puff out the opening.

Earthstars are related to puffballs and release their spores in the same way. This mushroom gets its common name from an outer covering that splits open to form a star around the ball-shaped fruiting body.

20

This species of earthstar *(Astraeus hygrometricus)* has an unusual checkered pattern on the outer layer that forms its star. Moisture causes the star to open (1), but when the mushroom becomes dry, the star closes up around the ball containing the spores (2). This pressure causes the spores to shoot out the hole in the top of the ball (3).

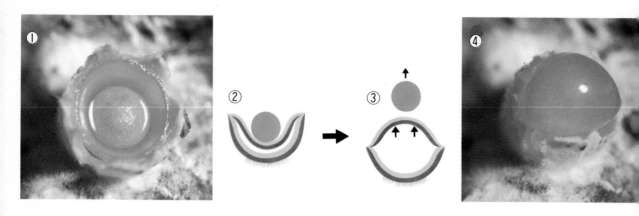

Another relative of the puffball is a tiny mushroom with the Latin name *Sphaerobolus.* The name means "sphere thrower," and it describes the way in which this unusual mushroom releases its spores. Like the puffball and the earthstar, *Sphaerobolus* has a spore mass inside its round fruiting body. Instead of puffing out its spores, however, the sphere thrower shoots out the whole spore mass.

The fruiting body of this amazing mushroom is made up of several different layers, one on top of the other. As the mushroom grows, the outermost layer splits open, revealing the yellowish spore mass inside (picture 1, above). Under the spore mass are two more layers that are attached to each other only at the edges (2). When the spores are ripe, the innermost layer suddenly springs up and flings the spore mass out, sometimes as much as 10 feet (about 3 meters) away from the fruiting body (3). After the spore mass is gone, the inner layer remains attached to the layer below it, bulging out like a shiny pink bubble (4).

22

Flies and other insects help the stinkhorn to scatter its spores.

The stinkhorn (right) also has an unusual way of releasing its spores. The young fruiting body of a stinkhorn develops inside an egg-shaped covering. When the fruiting body is mature, it breaks through the egg and shoots up to form a long, horn-like stalk. At the top of the stalk is a slimy, bad-smelling substance containing the mushroom's spores. The stinkhorn's unpleasant smell attracts flies and other insects that eat the spore-containing substance or get it on their feet. The insects carry the spores away, rubbing them off on trees and plants or scattering them in their droppings.

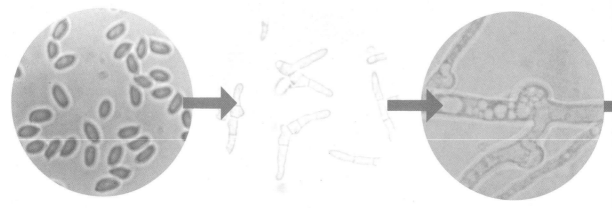

Left: Mushroom spores magnified about 1,000 times. Center: The spores begin to grow by sending out hyphae. Right: Hyphae from two different spores join together.

What happens to a spore after it is released from the fruiting body of a mushroom? Most of the millions of spores produced by a mushroom are lost or destroyed, but some survive to develop into new mushrooms. The process of that development is complicated and fascinating.

If a spore lands in a place where there is enough food and moisture, then it will begin to grow by sending out a tiny thread, or hypha. This one hypha quickly branches out and soon forms the mass of threads, or hyphae, that make up a mushroom's mycelium. The mycelium contains cells that take in nourishment and use it as fuel for continued growth.

The mycelium that grows from a single mushroom spore does not have the cells needed to produce a fruiting body. In order for this to happen, mycelia from two different spores must join together. This union is a form of **sexual reproduction,** similar in some ways to the uniting of male and female sex cells in animals and green plants.

24

The button of a fruiting body breaks through the surface of a dead tree.

Three days later, the cap and stalk have taken shape.

Five days after it first appeared, the fruiting body is fully developed.

Below: The hyphae become thick and knotted as they prepare to form fruiting bodies.

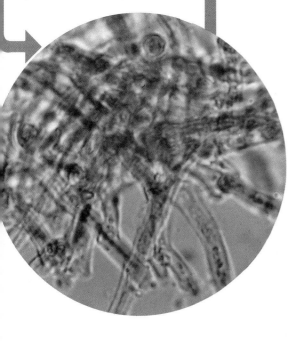

Mushroom mycelia cannot be identified as male or female, but there are two kinds of mycelia with different sets of characteristics. We could call them *A* mycelia and *B* mycelia. When the hyphae of an *A* mycelium join with the hyphae of a *B* mycelium, a new kind of growth begins to take place. Cells from the two mycelia unite to form the first stages of a fruiting body. This reproductive part of the mushroom contains the material that will produce spores, which will in turn produce a new generation of mushrooms.

The fruiting body of this mushroom has sprouted from a rotten log. The bark has been peeled away so that you can see the mycelium within the tissue of the log.

Like all plants and animals, mushrooms must have food in order to grow and reproduce. Green plants manufacture their own food by combining energy from sunlight with water, minerals, and the gas carbon dioxide. The leaves of green plants contain a material called **chlorophyll** that absorbs sunlight. Mushrooms and other fungi have no chlorophyll, so they cannot use the sun's energy to make food. Like animals, they must use food already manufactured by green plants.

Most mushrooms get their food from dead plants. The tiny threads of a mushroom's mycelium spread through a tree stump or a rotten log, absorbing the food energy stored in the dead wood.

26

Right: Mushroom mycelia growing on dead leaves. Below: Tiny mushrooms on the stem of a leaf. The tissue of the leaf is being gradually used as food for the mushroom.

Mushrooms find nourishment in dead trees (left) and in the decaying plant material buried in the earth of the forest floor (below).

Above and opposite: Tiny mushrooms in the genus *Marasmius* growing on dead wood

The mushrooms that grow on the dead plants of the forest are playing a role in an important cycle of natural life. They are acting as **decomposers,** breaking down the plant material into simpler forms. As the mushroom mycelia absorb the food energy stored in rotting trees and logs, they release minerals and other nutrients into the soil. The process of decomposition also produces the gas carbon dioxide. These materials are in turn used by green plants to manufacture new food.

The honey mushroom *(Armillaria mellea)* grows on both dead and living plants.

Some mushrooms get their nourishment from living plants rather than dead ones. Such mushrooms are known as **parasites.** When they begin to grow on a living tree, their mycelia send out chemicals that start the process of decomposition. As the mycelia grow larger and produce fruiting bodies, the decomposition spreads. Eventually the tree dies. The picture on the opposite page shows a tree that has been killed by a large number of wood-rotting mushrooms *(Panellus stipicus).*

32

Parasitic mushrooms are often found growing in some very strange places. A few kinds of mushrooms are parasites on other mushrooms. Their mycelia grow inside another mushroom's fruiting body, absorbing the nourishment it contains. As the parasites develop, their fruiting bodies sprout out of the other mushroom, as can be seen in the picture on the left.

Some earth tongue mushrooms are parasites not on plants but on animals. These mushrooms grow on the bodies of moths and other insects in the pupal stage of development (opposite). Inside its shell, a moth pupa goes through the process of changing into an adult insect. But if a pupa is attacked by a parasitic earth tongue, then its body will be used as food for the mushroom and it will die before becoming an adult.

34

This species of earth tongue *(Cordyceps militaris)* is called the military club because of its shape. In the picture above, the fruiting bodies of the military clubs seem to be growing in dead leaves. But when the leaves are cleared away, as in the photograph on the right, you can see one of the mushrooms sprouting out of a moth pupa.

A fairy ring in a wooded area

Whether they grow on an insect pupa, a living tree, or a rotten log, mushrooms have a significant effect on the natural environment. One of the strangest ways in which they affect the environment is through the formation of fairy rings.

A **fairy ring** is a circle of light-colored grass or plant growth that can be seen in a lawn, a meadow, or a forest. Around the outside of the light-colored circle is often a circle of mushroom fruiting bodies. People in the past called such strange formations fairy rings because they thought that the light-colored areas were caused by fairies who danced in circles during the dark of the night. Today scientists know that these rings are actually caused by the growth patterns of mushroom mycelia.

As mycelia grow, they spread out in a circular pattern. The edge of the circle is where the most active growth is taking place. As the mycelia in that area prepare to form fruiting bodies, they become very dense and thick. The closely packed hyphae absorb the nutrients and moisture in the soil, affecting the growth of the green plants in the area. The plants wither and die, forming the light-colored fairy ring.

This drawing shows how mushroom mycelia spread out in a circular pattern under the earth.

After the mycelia have produced fruiting bodies, they too die. The decaying mycelia enrich the soil inside the circle, and green plants begin to grow thickly there. But at the edge of the circle, new mycelia are growing from spores produced by the fruiting bodies. As these mycelia go through their cycle of development, another fairy ring appears. Over a period of time, the ring will appear again and again, becoming larger each time. Some fairy rings are known to have existed for several hundred years. One ring in England is believed to be around 700 years old!

A section of a large fairy ring formed by parasol mushrooms in the genus *Macrolepiota*. Many different kinds of mushrooms are known to produce these circular growth patterns. One species — *Marasmius oreades* — has been given the common name fairy ring musroom because it is so often seen in fairy rings.

Mold growing on a tree stump

When you see a fairy ring in a meadow or forest, you can be sure that mushrooms are living and growing there. Many other kinds of fungi grow all around us, but we are usually unaware of their presence.

Fungi such as molds and mildews are very much like mushrooms. Most of them have mycelia and fruiting bodies that produce spores. In fact, the basic difference between a mushroom and a fungus like the mold shown on the next page is that the mold has very small fruiting bodies that can be seen only through a microscope. Just like a mushroom, a mold or mildew takes its nourishment from the material in which it grows. In the process of absorbing food, the mycelium of the fungus sends out chemicals that break down the material and cause decomposition.

Many molds and mildews play a useful role as decomposers in the natural world, just as mushrooms do. But some of these fungi are destructive, attacking living plants and doing a great deal of damage. Plant diseases such as potato blight and wheat rust are caused by parasitic fungi that spread rapidly and destroy food crops. A few fungi even act as parasites on human beings, causing skin diseases like athlete's foot and ringworm.

Left: Mold growing on a piece of cake. Below: In this photograph, the mold has been magnified 80 times so that you can see the threads of the mycelium and the fruiting bodies.

This cherry tree is infected with a parasitic fungus that causes the branches to wither and die. The photograph in the circle shows the fungus magnified 400 times.

Other kinds of fungi have proved to be very beneficial to humans. The one-celled fungi called **yeasts** are used to make bread, alcoholic beverages, and other foods. This kind of fungi causes **fermentation,** a process that breaks down sugars into carbon dioxide and alcohol. Some fungi have been used to produce medicines that cure human diseases. The important antibiotic penicillin is made from a mold that belongs to the genus *Penicillium.* Other modern medicines used to treat a variety of diseases are also produced from fungi.

Opposite: The oyster mushroom *(Pleurotus ostreatus)* is one of the delicious edible mushrooms common in many parts of North America.

Many kinds of fungi have played important roles in human life, but the fungus that human beings know best is the mushroom. For thousands of years, people have collected wild mushrooms of all kinds and have used them as food. Today mushroom collecting is still a very popular pastime in many parts of the world.

Many of the mushrooms that grow wild in the fields and forests of North America make good food and are safe to eat. But some wild mushrooms are poisonous, causing sickness and even death if they are eaten.

If you are interested in collecting wild mushrooms, it is very important to know how to recognize the poisonous species. There are no general rules that you can use to tell edible mushrooms from poisonous ones. Mushroom collectors learn to identify mushrooms by knowing the individual characteristics of each species. A good field guide will give you the information you need to begin learning about mushroom identification.

Identifying mushrooms can be fascinating even if you are not interested in collecting and eating the fungi. By learning to recognize some of the different kinds of mushrooms, you will discover how varied and beautiful these strange plants can be.

About the Names Used in This Book

Like all plants and animals, mushrooms have several different kinds of names. The mushrooms in this book are usually referred to by their **common names.** These are ordinary English names that often describe the mushroom's appearance or some other characteristic. For example, parasol mushrooms look like tiny umbrellas, while the mushroom known as the destroying angel is pure white in color and contains a deadly poison.

Such names are fascinating, but they can be a source of confusion. It often happens that one kind of mushroom will have different common names in the different regions where it grows. When a mushroom grows in several different countries, it will have a common name in the language of each country, and these names may be completely unlike one another.

Since common names vary so much from place to place, people who study mushrooms usually call the plants by their **scientific names.** Each kind of mushroom has a two-part name in Latin that is known and used by scientists all over the world. For example, the scientific name of the destroying angel is *Amanita virosa.* This name not only identifies the mushroom but also tells something about its relationship with other kinds of mushrooms.

When scientists identify a particular mushroom by a scientific name, they are placing it in a group of plants that share the same special features. This group, known as a **species,** is the basic unit in the system of scientific classification. The destroying angel belongs to the species *Amanita virosa;* other mushrooms similar to the destroying angel but with slightly different characteristics belong to other species. For example, the fly mushroom belongs to the species *Amanita muscaria,* while the beautiful orange Caesar's mushroom is in the species *Amanita caesarea.* All of these species are part of a larger group in the system of classification known as a **genus.** The first part of a species name identifies the mushroom's genus. As you can see, the destroying angel, the fly mushroom, and Caesar's mushroom are all members of the genus *Amanita.*

In this book, mushrooms will be identified by their genus or species names as well as their common names. These Latin names are important not only to scientists but also to anyone who wants to learn about the natural world.

Like common names, scientific names often describe a mushroom's appearance or some other characteristic. *Amanita virosa* (right) got its name because of its poisonous nature. *Virosa* comes from the Latin *virus*, meaning "poison."

Above: If you know that the scientific name of the morel is *Morchella esculenta*, then you know that this mushroom is good to eat. *Esculenta* is the Latin word for "edible." Right: This mushroom is called the tree ear in English. Its scientific name, *Auricularia auricula*, also refers to its ear-like shape. Both parts of the name come from *auris*, the Latin word for "ear."

GLOSSARY

annulus (AN-yuh-lus) — the ring on the stalk of a mushroom formed by the broken veil

cap — the upper part of an umbrella-shaped mushroom

chlorophyll (KLOR-uh-fill) — a substance in green plants that absorbs sunlight. Chlorophyll makes it possible for green plants to manufacture their own food.

decomposers — plants or animals that cause organic material to be broken down into simpler forms

fairy ring — a circle of light-colored plant growth often accompanied by a circle of mushroom fruiting bodies

fermentation — a process that breaks down sugars into carbon dioxide and alcohol

fruiting body — the part of a mushroom that produces spores

fungi (FUN-ji or FUN-gi) — simple plants that cannot make their own food because they lack chlorophyll. Mushrooms, molds, mildews, and yeasts are all fungi. The singular form of the word is *fungus* (FUN-guhs).

gills — thin ridges on the undersides of the caps of some mushrooms. Spores are produced on the surface of the gills.

hyphae (HI-fee) — thread-like rows of cells that make up a mushroom mycelium and fruiting body. The singular form of the word is *hypha* (HI-fuh).

mycelium (my-SEEL-ee-um) — a mass of thread-like structures that forms the main part of a mushroom. The plural form of the word is *mycelia* (my-SEEL-ee-uh).

46

parasites (PAIR-uh-sites)—plants or animals that get their nourishment from other living things

pores—tiny holes on the spore-producing surfaces of some mushrooms

sexual reproduction—a form of reproduction in which new life is formed by the union of cells from two different individuals

spores—tiny cells produced by mushroom fruiting bodies that can develop into new mushrooms

spore mass—a structure that contains the spores produced inside the fruiting bodies of some mushrooms

spore prints—images formed on paper by the spores of some kinds of mushrooms. Scientists can identify these mushrooms by the patterns and colors of their spore prints.

universal veil—a thin skin that encloses a developing Amanita mushroom. As the mushroom grows, the universal veil breaks, forming a cup at the base of the stalk.

veil—a thin skin that protects the gills of a developing mushroom. As the mushroom grows, the veil breaks, forming a ring on the stalk.

yeasts—one-celled fungi that cause fermentation

INDEX

Amanita mushrooms, 9, 10-11, 12, 18, 43
annulus, 9, 14

Boletus mushrooms, 16, 17, 19
bracket mushrooms, 16

cap, mushroom, 9
chlorophyll, 26
collecting mushrooms, 42, 44

decomposers, fungi as, 30, 41
diseases caused by fungi, 41

earthstars, 20, 21, 23
earth tongues, 7, 34, 35
edible mushrooms, 42, 44

fairy rings, 36-37, 38
fermentation, 42
food used by mushrooms, 26, 30, 32, 34
fruiting body, 8, 36, 37, 39; development of, 8-9, 24, 25, 34; spore production in, 12, 16, 20, 22, 23
fungi, 5, 26, 39, 41-42

gilled mushrooms, 12, 14, 18
gills, 12, 13, 14, 15, 16
green plants, 5, 26

Hydnum (genus), 16
hyphae, 8, 13, 24, 25, 37

inky cap mushroom, 14-15

medicines made from fungi, 42
mildews, 39, 41
molds, 39, 41, 42
mycelium, 8, 13, 26, 30, 32, 41; development of, 24-25, 34; growth patterns of, 36-37

parasites, mushrooms as, 32, 34, 35, 41
penicillin, 42
poisonous mushrooms, 10, 42, 44
pores, 16
potato blight, 41
puffballs, 20, 22

reproduction, 24-25
ringworm, 41

shelf fungi, 7, 16, 17
Sphaerobolus, 22
sphere-thrower mushroom, 22
spore mass, 20, 22
spore prints, 16, 18
spores, 13, 14, 18; growth of, 24-25; production of, 12, 16; release of, 12, 15, 20-23
stinkhorn mushrooms, 20, 23

table mushroom, common, 14
teethed mushrooms, 16

universal veil, 9

veil, 9

wheat rust, 41
wood-rotting mushrooms, 32

yeasts, 42